This book is dedicated to my brother,
who always makes me laugh.

ACKNOWLEDGEMENTS

I thank Mom for her love, encouragement, and support. I also thank renowned author Dallas Woodburn for reviewing and editing my writing.

Rosalie Chiang

We thank Wayne Ho and Rommel Yuan for their excellent technical assistance. We thank Benjamin Twist (booby), Samuel Blanc (penguin), Dario Sanches (xenops), Alan Vernon (yellowhammer), and Jim Bendon (zebra finch) for granting us permission to make derivative works from their photographs. We thank Dick Daniels (ostrich) and Donar Reiskoffer (toucan) for making their photographs available under a Creative Commons license. We acknowledge the following famous 19th century naturalists/artists whose paintings from which many of our pictures are based on: John James Audubon (albatross, cardinal, eagle, flamingo, goose, hummingbird, ibis, jay, quail, spoonbill, and vulture), Francis Orpen Morris (duck), Lorenz Oken (kiwi), Edward Lear (macaw), James Bolton (nightingale), and Joseph Wolf Lichter (umbrellabird).

Robin & Rosalie Chiang

Then God said, "... let birds fly above the earth ..."
Genesis 1:20 (NKJV)

European Buzzard, drawn by Robin Chiang at age 7

 is for Albatross.

Albatross, slender and sleek
Catching fish with its hooked beak
Swallowing whole tail and fin
On its wings it rides the wind.

The albatross is found on all continents except Europe. It feeds on squid and fish. Some can have a wingspan of up to eleven feet and have a life span of up to fifty years. Similar to some other sea birds, it drinks salt water.

A is for Albatross
~ Birds A to Z ~

by Rosalie Chiang

Illustrated by Robin & Rosalie Chiang

A Chiang Publication

 is for Booby.

The blue-footed booby bird
Strangest bird I've ever heard
Webbed feet and beak are blue
They sure are a pretty hue.

The blue-footed booby lives in Central and South America. It feeds on small fish such as anchovies. During mating season, the male boobies do a high-stepping strut to show off their blue webbed feet.

 is for Cardinal.

Cardinal, bright chili red
Wears a black mask on its head
And its wings are reddish gray
Flies high like Santa's sleigh.

The Northern Cardinal lives in the eastern United States and Mexico. It eats seeds, fruits, and insects. Both the female and male sing. It is named after the cardinals of the Roman Catholic Church who wear all red.

 is for Duck.

Beautiful harlequin duck
Gliding through the pond and muck
Body orange, black, and blue
Pretty white stripes running through.

The harlequin duck is a sea duck found mainly in northwest and northeast North America. It eats snails, crabs, fish roe, and insects. Males are brightly colored while females are brownish-grey. It is also called a "sea mouse" or "squeaker" because it makes a high-pitched call.

 is for Eagle.

Golden eagle, strong and brown
Flying sunup to sundown
Feathers spread out brown and black
Talons ready to attack.

The golden eagle lives in North America, Asia, and Europe. Its diet includes rabbits, squirrels, reptiles, birds, and fish. It can dive up to a speed of 150 miles per hour. It is the national bird of Mexico.

 is for Flamingo.

Flamingo, clothed fully pink
Tip of beak is black as ink
Its neck is curved and so long
Thin legs look weak but are strong.

The greater flamingo lives in Africa, Asia, and the Caribbean. Its diet is plankton, tiny fish, and insect larvae. Its pink coloration comes from eating many crustaceans containing a pink pigment. The chicks are born gray and white.

 is for Goose.

Canada goose with black feet
Its ducklings are quite petite
Black wings widely it does spread
With a dark beak on its head.

The Canada goose lives in North America and Europe. Its diet is grass, grain, and berries. It lives in flocks, and migrates south during the winter in magnificent V-formations.

 is for Hummingbird.

Green Columbian hummingbird
Moves so fast, its wings are blurred
Its red head is very bright
Flitting quickly out of sight.

The Columbian hummingbird, also known as Anna's hummingbird, is found on the west coast of North America. It feeds on nectar and small insects. It is only about four inches long.

 is for Ibis.

American white ibis
Snowy white, one cannot miss
Its orange beak is quite bright
The adult is very light.

The American white Ibis lives along the coast of the southern United States. It eats crayfish, insects and small fish. An adult only weighs about two pounds. Native American tradition says that the ibis seeks shelter last before a hurricane, and comes out first afterwards.

 is for Jay.

O blue jay, pretty blue jay
Such a beautiful display
Catching bugs with pointed beak
Pulling worms with great technique.

The blue jay is found in North America. It feeds on acorns, nuts, seeds, insects, and sometimes eggs. It is a social bird, and most migrate south for the winter.

 is for Kiwi.

Kiwi truly is unique
How it sports its long curved beak
Always very feathery
Northern Island brown kiwi.

The North Island brown kiwi lives in New Zealand. It eats seeds, bugs, fruits, crayfish, eels, and amphibians. It is usually nocturnal, and lays the biggest egg in proportion to its size. It is the national symbol of New Zealand.

 is for Lark.

Horned lark with belly so white
With glee it soars in flight
Face masked yellow, white, and black
Don't forget its dark brown back.

The horned lark lives in North America, Europe, and Asia. It eats seeds and insects, and can have a clutch of five eggs. Its name comes from the distinctive feather pattern of black "horns" which the males develop in summer.

 is for Macaw.

Scarlet macaw, super bright
Squawking on throughout the night
Feathers blue, red, and yellow
Eating fruits and staying mellow.

The scarlet macaw is found in Central and South America. It feeds on fruits, nuts, and seeds. The adult grows to about thirty-two inches long and has a lifespan of up to seventy-five years in captivity. It is the national bird of Honduras.

 is for Nightingale.

Petite common nightingale
With its long, brown, pretty tail
Flying, jumping to and fro
Singing to all down below.

The common nightingale is found in Europe, Asia, and Africa. It is about six inches long. It frequently sings at night, which led to its Old English name meaning "night songstress." Its songs have been described as the most beautiful in nature, and are the inspiration of songs, stories, and operas.

 is for Ostrich.

Regal ostrich, swift and tall
The biggest bird of them all
Body feathers black and white
Its bare neck is quite all right.

The ostrich is found only in Africa. It is the world's largest bird. Though it cannot fly, it is a fast runner, capable of speeds of forty miles per hour. Contrary to popular depiction, it does not put its head in the ground.

 is for Penguin.

Emperor Penguin, standing tall
Snow-swept landscape held in awe
Blackish backs and tummies white
Flocks of thousands, what a sight!

The emperor penguin lives in Antarctica. It feeds on fish, squid, and krill. It is flightless and an adult stands up to forty-eight inches tall. It is the largest penguin in the world. Each mating season, the female lays a single egg, while the male incubates it by balancing it on its feet.

 is for Quail.

Dear Californian quail
Rainbow body, short grey tail
Bright feathers upon its head
Running around, keeping fed.

The Californian quail lives in the western United States and Mexico. It feeds on berries, insects, seeds, and leaves. If startled, it will fight. The female lays about twelve eggs. It is the state bird of California.

 is for Roadrunner.

Swift roadrunner, very tan
Look how quickly it just ran
Lots of feathers sticking out
On brown feet it runs about.

The greater roadrunner lives in the deserts of the southwestern United States and Mexico. It eats small mammals, invertebrates, and reptiles. It can run up to twenty miles per hour. It is the state bird of New Mexico.

 is for Spoonbill.

Roseate spoonbill comes and goes
Tummy, wings, and feet are rose
Its brown and blue spoon-like bill
Scoops up food with lots of skill.

The roseate spoonbill lives in the coastal regions of the Caribbean in North and South America. Its diet is mainly fish and other aquatic animals. It nests in trees and lays two to five eggs in each clutch.

 is for Toucan.

Keel-billed toucan, feet of blue
Body has a blackish hue
Blue-ringed eyes set in yellow
Its great beak, colored rainbow.

The keeled-billed toucan lives in Central and South America. Its diet is fruits, lizards, eggs, young birds, and insects. Its beak can grow up to six inches long. It builds its nest in tree holes, and is the national bird of Belize.

 is for Umbrellabird.

O bare-necked umbrellabird
Certainly looks quite absurd
Wearing an umbrella cap
Wattle feathers overlap.

The bare-necked umbrellabird is found in the rainforests of Costa Rica and Panama. It feeds on fruits, insects, and lizards. It can grow up to sixteen inches long. It is solitary and has a loud, booming call.

 is for Vulture.

Turkey Vulture! Scary sight!
Body dark as a moonless night
Look at its red bald head
Eats animals that are dead.

The turkey vulture is found in North America. It scavenges by feeding on dead animals. It nests on the ground. It is named because, from a distance, it resembles a turkey.

 is for Woodpecker.

Ivory-billed woodpecker
A sharp beak to peck in firs
Tips of wings and neck are white
Its sharp eyes are full of light.

The ivory-billed woodpecker, found only in the United States, has been considered critically endangered since the 1940s. It pecks on trees to find food, such as beetle larvae. It is the largest woodpecker in the world. Since 2004, sightings of the bird in Arkansas and Florida have been reported.

 is for Xenops.

Streaked xenops, clothed in coffee
Climbing all around its tree
With its stubby blue-gray beak
It calls out its winsome squeak.

The streaked xenops lives in South and Central America. It eats insects and sometimes steals prey from other birds. It is a tree-creeper, which means it likes to climb around tree trunks.

 is for Yellowhammer.

Yellowhammer, feathered friend
On the branch all day it spends
Gaily singing in the breeze
"Lil' bit of bread and no cheese!"

The yellowhammer is found in Europe and Russia. It eats seeds, food plants, and grain. It likes to sit on an anthill and catch ants by letting them crawl on its wings. Its song sounds like it is saying: "A little bit of bread and no cheese."

 is for Zebra Finch.

O zebra finch, flying free
Hopping around from tree to tree
Orange feathers with white dots
Blackish tail with snow-white spots.

The colorful zebra finch is mainly found in Australia, and has been introduced into other continents. It feeds on seeds and fresh food. It prefers living in drier areas.

BIBLIOGRAPHY

1. John James Audubon, *The Birds of America*, 1827-1838.
2. James Bolton, *Harmonia Ruralis: An Essay Towards a Natural History of British Song Birds and Their Nests*, 1845.
3. Edward Lear, *Illustrations of the Family of Psittacidae, or Parrots*, 1832.
4. Joseph Wolf Lichter, *Proceedings of the Zoological Society of London*, 1850.
5. Francis Orpen Morris, *A History of British Birds*, 1850-1857.
6. Lorenz Oken, *Naturgeschichte für alle Stände (Natural History for all Social Ranks)*, 1843.
7. www.nationalgeographic.com.
8. www.wikipedia.org.

ABOUT THE AUTHOR AND ILLUSTRATOR

Rosalie Chiang is a ten-year-old growing up in the San Francisco Bay Area with her parents and brother. She has won several awards for poetry and writing. Her interests are biology, acting, writing poetry, gardening, and cooking. This is her first book.

Robin Chiang is Rosalie's father, and is an attorney at law with a Ph.D. in Microbiology & Molecular Genetics. He is interested in a wide variety of topics ranging from biofuels to phaleristics.

Made in the USA
Middletown, DE
18 November 2016